The **Essential** Buyer's Guide

HARLEY-DAVIDSON
Big Twins

FL, FX/Softail and Dyna series
1340cc, 1450cc, 1584cc, 1690cc, 1800cc
1984-2010

Your marque expert:
Peter Hensh

VELOCE PUBLISHING
THE PUBLISHER OF FINE AUTOMOTIVE BOOKS

Also from Veloce –

From Veloce Publishing's new imprints:

BATTLE CRY!

Hubble & **Hattie**

www.veloce.co.uk

First published in March 2011 by Veloce Publishing Limited, Veloce House, Parkway Farm Business Park, Middle Farm Way, Poundbury, Dorchester, Dorset, DT1 3AR, England. Fax 01305 250479/ e-mail info@veloce.co.uk/web www.veloce.co.uk or www.velocebooks.com.

ISBN: 978-1-845843-03-8 UPC:6-36847-04303-2

British Library Cataloguing in Publication Data – A catalogue record for this book is available from the British Library. Typesetting, design and page make-up all by Veloce Publishing Ltd on Apple Mac. Printed in India by Replika Press.

Introduction
– the purpose of this book

Harley-Davidson Big Twins are revered by some, loathed by others, but whatever you think of them, these are the original big V-twin, offering a riding experience unlike that of any other bike, even though some Japanese cruisers come close. What's different about a Harley is that name on the tank, which brings with it 100 years of history, images of the great American road trip, of Lee Marvin in *The Wild One* and Dennis Hopper in *Easy Rider*. Whichever model you go for, it's very much a feel good motorcycle, and there's nothing quite like the lazy beat of that big V-twin on a perfect summer's day.

This book is a straightforward, practical guide to buying a big Harley secondhand. It won't list all the correct colour combinations for each year, or delve into the minutae of year-by-year changes – there are excellent books and magazines that do all of this. Hopefully though, it will help you avoid buying a lemon.

What it won't do is look at the pre-1983 bikes. The Evolution engine, launched in late '83, was a great leap forward in reliability and oil tightness from its rough and ready forbears. If you're looking at your first Harley, it's good to start with one of these, or the 2000-on Twin Cam, simply because they're far less hassle to own. Of course, if you do get bitten by the Harley bug (and many do) then you might want to chase a more collectible Shovelhead or Panhead later on. But in terms of something

Buy a Big Twin, and you buy a slice of motorcycle history.

that delivers the H-D experience, while starting on the button and not leaving oil stains on the garage floor, an Evo or Twin Cam is the bike to have.

By any modern standards of performance, braking, and (fully dressed tourers aside) comfort, even these bikes are well behind the times. But as any Harley rider will tell you, that isn't really the point. It's the riding experience that counts, and in a world where speed is under increasing restriction, they can make a lot of sense.

'96 cubic inches' – a world where bigger is seen as better.

Some people insist that all Harley Big Twins are the same, and they're certainly all based around the same basic engine and gearbox. But there are distinctions – the company realised long ago that it was possible to offer a range of different bikes by changing the frame, suspension, bodywork, seat, fuel tank and a host of other things. So a Heritage Softail is distinct from a Road Glide, which in turn is quite different to an FXR Super Glide.

Whichever Harley you choose, if you don't get on with it, they are quite easy to sell on, and because they hold their value, you shouldn't lose much in the transaction. Not everyone likes them, but it's worth taking the time to acclimatise – many official dealers offer hire schemes, so you can have a test ride over a few days to really get the feel of the bike. And if you do get bitten by the Harley bug, you're affected for life.

This book could not have been written without the help of Harvey King at H-D dealer Riders of Bridgwater. Thanks also go to the Dyna Glide rider at the Clay Pigeon, and to the owners of bikes I photographed while they were away!

Official dealers have a good range of new and used bikes.

Essential Buyer's Guide™ currency

At the time of publication a BG unit of currency "●" equals approximately £1.00/US$1.50/Euro 1.20. Please adjust to suit current exchange rates.

Contents

1 Is it the right bike for you?
– marriage guidance

The low seat compensates for high weight.

Tall and short riders
Harleys are heavy, but they're more suitable for short riders than you might think, with seat heights from just over 600mm. And there's still plenty of space for six-footers to stretch out. Just don't forget these bikes can weigh 300kg or more.

Running costs
Big bikes cost big money to run, and Harleys are no exception. Fuel consumption can dip below 40mpg when ridden hard, and insurance is high. On the other hand, tyres last well and a 5000-mile service costs ●x220 at a Harley dealer (at time of writing).

Maintenance
Easy, especially on Twin Cams. The belt drive is maintenance-free, and oil/filter

changes are every 5000 miles. Hydraulic tappets adjust themselves, so owners just need to keep an eye on tyres (5-10,000-mile life) and brake pads. Evos also need a 2500-mile checkover service.

Usability
Better than you might think. Keep on top of the cosmetics (there's a lot of chrome to polish) and some models are usable all year round – stress-free to ride, lowish maintenance and (in the case of the tourers) comfortable.

Parts availability
Excellent, whether from Harley dealers or the many independent specialists. Applies to both standard parts and the huge array of accessories.

Parts costs
Not cheap, though thanks to the simple routine maintenance there's not much to buy for regular servicing – just oil, filters, plugs and (eventually) a drive belt.

Insurance group
High, because Harleys are expensive bikes, not to mention very stealable. Many are kept in urban areas, which doesn't help. Look for a limited-mileage insurance policy. Early Evos may qualify for classic bike policies.

Investment potential
There are too many Harley Big Twins around to make them a good investment, but they do hold their value better than any comparable bike. New Harleys suffer in their first two to three years, but values then level out and (given normal low mileage) hardly drop any more. This is virtually unique among secondhand bikes, and at least means that if you don't get on with a Harley, and it's still in the same condtion you bought it in, you can resell it for a similar price.

Foibles
It's the badge. The Harley-Davidson name is the most recognisable in motorcycling, and comes with a lot of baggage. Some people love the badge and all that goes with it, others don't.

Plus points
Easy to ride and maintain; big, gruff, laidback V-twin; feels like it's built to last 100 years; very active club scene, with both HOG and independent clubs; gets you noticed.

Minus points
Gets you noticed; very heavy (as are all big cruisers); stealable and not cheap to run; slow (in standard form) by modern standards; limited ground clearance.

Alternatives
The whole raft of Japanese cruisers that look and sound very like Harleys, but don't quite get there: Honda VTX1800, Kawasaki VN1600/2000, Suzuki VZR1800, Yamaha XV1700/1900. For something different, look at Moto Guzzi's California, Triumph's Thunderbird 1600, or the BMW R1200C.

2 Cost considerations
– affordable, or a money pit?

Harleys cost a lot to buy and run. Servicing costs aren't too bad, at ⬤x60-70 for a 2500-mile check, and ⬤x220 for a 5000-mile – these are official dealer prices. But the bikes *are* gas guzzlers. A gentle rider might manage as much as 50mpg, but 35-45mpg is more typical, and injected bikes are better than carb ones. Tyres last well, up to 10,000 miles from a set, given solo riding and sub-freeway speeds, but insurance costs are high, thanks to spares prices (see below) the bikes' value, and stealability. Look around for a limited mileage policy. Spares prices here are from an official Harley dealer – exact prices will vary according to model.

Complete restoration (basket case to concours) – around ⬤15,000.

Tyres last well.

Air filter (K&N) ⬤x50
Air filter (stage 1 kit) ⬤x131
Alternator (32 amp) ⬤x225
Battery ⬤x80
Big bore kit (103in³) ⬤x510
Brake calipers (4-pot, pr) ⬤x225
Brake disc ⬤x150
Brake pads (front) ⬤x20
Clutch cable assy ⬤x41
Drive belt ⬤x250
Fork assy complete ⬤x850
Fork stanchion ⬤x101
Fuel tank ⬤x494
Handlebar switch ⬤x73
Headlight shell ⬤x61
Oil change kit (engine/gearbox/filter) ⬤x49
Oil pump/billet cam plate ⬤x403
Primary chain ⬤x73
Regulator ⬤x67
Seat ⬤x187
Silencer ⬤x120
Sparkplugs (pr) ⬤x8
Speedometer cable ⬤x140
Starter motor ⬤x337
Tyre (front) ⬤x80
Tyre (rear) ⬤x130

The toothed belt is a positive bonus, reducing maintenance.

Parts can be expensive.

If you've decided you want a Harley-Davidson, then you are unlikely to change your mind. It's probably the most aspirational bike in the world, and wanting to own one often precludes any more practical considerations. That said, there are some things to think about before going ahead and buying a Big Twin.

First of all, these are big, heavy bikes that need careful manoevring at low speed. They're not actually that difficult to ride, but smaller people do need to bear in mind their sheer mass when parking. If you think the weight might be too much, look at the Sportster instead, which offers much the same Harley experience in a smaller, lighter package. On all Harleys, the clutch is heavier than on smaller machines, the gear-change slower and more deliberate – they respond to a different riding style to that of the average 600cc supersport.

On the other hand, as 250-300kg

You might not get on with this particular bike, but there are plenty of different machines to choose from.

bikes go, the Big Twins are relatively easy to manage. They are big and wide, but the seats are very low – little more than 600mm on some Softails, to a maximum of 700mm. And the V-twin is very forgiving, happy to chug along at low speed for as long as you like. Fuel-injected bikes have the most seamless manners of all.

Big V-twins vibrate, there's no getting away from that, though the rubber mounting system used on all Evo and Twin Cam Harleys (Softails excepted) works very well over 2000rpm, effectively quelling the vibes. You're left in no doubt that there's a big engine shuddering away underneath, but it's all in the background. The Softail does without the rubber mounts, and in 1984-99 Evo form, does deliver serious vibration. The Twin Cam Softail from 2000, with its balance shaft engine, is far better.

Motorcycling folklore insists that Harleys don't handle and have terrible brakes. It's true that the steering is slow, while cornering clearance varies from model to model (most FXRs and some Dynas are best, Softails are worst), but it's all adequate at normal cruising speeds. Ride a Harley hard on a twisty road, and these deficiencies will start to show up, but the bottom line is that they handle as well as other cruisers. Evo (pre-1999) brakes really aren't up to the performance, though many bikes will have been upgraded over the years. Twin Cam (1999/2000-on) brakes are fine.

Harley-Davidsons are not fast – Evos muster only around 52bhp at the rear wheel, and 88/96 Twin Cams about 62bhp, which isn't much for a 300kg bike. On the other hand, they have plenty of torque, and will effortlessly move around in top gear – that makes them a less stressful bike to ride than one with more power, but which demands more gearchanging. Many Japanese and European bikes encourage you to ride fast, but a Harley does the opposite, which in an increasingly frenetic world is a nice character trait. In standard form, most have a top speed of 95-105mph, though cruising speed is more dictated by the riding position than anything else – a Road Glide will be comfortable at 80-90mph, but hanging on to a Fat Boy with no screen at that speed takes a lot of determination!

If you insist, there are plenty of tuning parts to boost performance, including Harley's own Screamin' Eagle brand as well as countless other suppliers. The sky's the limit: everything from simple stage 1 kits – a more free-flowing exhaust and air filter – to radical big-capacity kits. Whatever the stage of tune, if the bike you're interested in has it, ask who did the work – a Harley dealer or independent specialist is good news – but really it's best to steer clear of radically tuned bikes. The Harley V-twin is a strong engine, but given sufficient abuse the crankcases can eventually crack.

Mechanically, these are simple bikes, and quite easy to look after. A few (all of them early Evos) use chain drive, but the vast majority are belt drive. The toothed belt does not need lubing or adjusting between tyre changes – just keep an eye on it for stone damage. Oil and filter changes come up every 5000 miles (Evos need a minor service at 2500) but there are no valve clearances to worry about, thanks to the hydraulic tappets. In standard form, these engines are understressed, so they last well, with 100,000 miles possible before major work is needed. Expect 7-10,000 miles from tyres (or less if you do lots of heavily-laden high speed miles) which is pretty good for a bike this heavy.

The Evo and Twin Cam are far easier to live with than earlier Harleys – more reliable, far less likely to leak oil, and with the vibration tamed in one way or another (Evo Softails apart). Some riders are still turned off by the negative associations of the Harley-Davidson badge, but you don't have to join a backpatch club, and some riders really do use them as all-year round transport, so they can't all be dismissed as Sunday-only rides. Either way, you will need to keep on top of the cleaning – these are naked bikes with lots of nooks, crannies and chrome, and they don't take kindly to cosmetic neglect.

If you really can't decide whether or not to take the plunge, then try before you buy. Harley dealerships offer a range of test bikes for demo rides, and many will even rent you one for a couple of days. That's the best way to find out whether you will get along together.

Belt drive is easy to live with.

See chapter 12 for value assessment. This chapter shows, in percentage terms, the value of individual models in good condition. This chapter looks at the strengths and weaknesses of each model, so that you can decide which is best for you.

At first sight, the Harley-Davidson system of model names and letters looks like an impenetrable jungle, especially as many different bikes look very similar to each other. But take heart, because it's not as complicated as it seems! Basically, there are three families: FL series (tourers), Softails (custom cruisers) and FXR/Dyna Glides (all-rounders). All three share many major components, such as the engine/gearbox, and there's lots of mix and matching across the range – a Fat Boy, for example, uses an FL front end with a Softail main frame.

Range availability

Evo & Twin Cam engines

First of all, let's get to the heart of every Harley Big Twin, the engine shared by every bike in this book. H-D has built V-twins since 1909, but the Evo (short for Evolution) launched 74 years later was a great leap forward. Older Harley twins vibrated and leaked oil – the Evo, though still an air-cooled pushrod engine, was quieter and better mannered. Vibration was tamed by

The Evolution engine was more of a revolution for H-D.

rubber mounting. It transformed the company's fortunes, selling to a new generation of riders who didn't want to get their hands dirty.

By modern standards, the 1340cc Evo is very simple: air cooling, carburettor (most bikes), two valves per cylinder, and pushrods (with hydraulic tappets). In standard form, power is restricted to around 52bhp at the rear wheel, so performance can seem sluggish. But even as standard, the Evo is a torquey engine, and has that rumbling big twin appeal that is central to any Harley. Fuel-injection, featuring gradually from 1995, brought smoother running, a more reliable idle, and automatic choke.

In 1999/2000, the Evo was superseded by the Twin Cam. This, too, was a 45-degree air-cooled V-twin, and even looks very similar to the engine it replaced – look for the bigger finning and oval (not round) air cleaner. But inside, there were some major changes, and H-D claimed that only 18 parts were interchangeable between the two.

The Twin Cam was a bigger engine at 1450cc (88in³), and had a shorter stroke, plus better breathing to give more power – about 62bhp at the rear wheel – and tuning potential. There were two camshafts instead of one, and the bottom end was strengthened. At first most Twin Cams used carbs, but fuel-injection was universal by 2003. There were two versions: TCA was fitted to bikes with rubber-mount frames (tourers and Dyna Glides) while TCB, with balance shafts to quell vibration, was bolted solidly into Softails.

For 2007, capacity was boosted to 1584cc (96in³) with improvements to cam bearings, cam chain tensioner and oil pump, plus many other changes – in fact, the engine was largely new. It came with the CruiseDrive six-speed gearbox, which reduced top gear rpm by 11 per cent, making the Harley even more of a relaxed cruiser. For 2009, CVO (Custom Vehicle Operations) bikes across the range came with an 1800cc (110in³) Twin Cam, and the following year the top touring FL in the standard range received a 1690cc (103in³) version.

The Twin Cam took over for the 21st century.

The Electra Glide makes a great tourer, for stress-free mile eating.

FL series – the tourers

The tourers are a good choice for distance, as capable of covering big miles in comfort as any modern tourer from BMW or the Japanese, unless you insist on three-figure cruising speeds. Fully dressed Electra Glides have loads of luggage room, rivalled only by a Goldwing or BMW LT. The riding position is comfortable all day, with a deep seat, big footboards, and pulled-back bars, while the fairngs, whether bar- or frame-mounted, keep the weather off very well. And at the heart of it all is a big-inch V-twin – what it lacks in outright power is made up for by torque and high gearing, enabling it to lope along all day without stressing itself or the rider. Pillions get a good deal on the FL series as well.

Pillion seats don't get much comfier than this.

Within the FL family, there are three subgroups: Electra Glide, Road Glide and Road King. The Electra Glide is the classic touring Harley, with traditional bar-mounted fairing, spotlights, panniers, and topbox. Electra Glides are often loaded with extras: full luggage, sound system, air suspension ... the list goes on and on. The Ultra Classic was the ultimate factory model, though many owners carried on adding equipment. When buying an Electra Glide, check that all the many accessories work.

The Road Glide, originally the FLT, was Harley's attempt to modernise the Electra Glide back in 1980, with a big squared-off fairing mounted on the frame instead of the bars. In theory, that should improve the handling, but whether that was true or not, in practice many more buyers preferred the classic look of the Electra. In any case, at least one road test of the FLT reckoned that the Electra's traditional bar fairing actually did a better job of weather protection. More recently, the Road Glide has been very similar in spec to the Electra Glide, and the choice between the two really comes down to which look you prefer. The Road

Full luggage comes with nearly all Electra Glides.

The Softail Springer is the ultimate in retro.

Glide is certainly the rarer bike, especially in the UK.

The 90th Anniversary FLs of 1993 are worth seeking out, as is the Ultra Classic Electra two years later, the first Big Twin with fuel-injection – that was a limited edition, before injection spread through the range the year after. Another variation was the FLHS Sport, basically an Electra with a screen instead of the fairing, and no top box. It wasn't a great success, but it spawned the Road King in 1993, which has created a following all of its own. There's much to recommend the Road King if you want the comfort of an FL tourer without a fairing – the screen is detachable. Some like the Street Glide too, offered since 2005: an Electra with a small screen for the long, low 'bagger' look.

The touring Harleys tend to be owned by contientious and knowledgeable people, often liable to use their bikes for long summer holidays. So mileages will often be higher than on other models, but given an understanding owner that's not necessarily a bad thing.

Strengths/weaknesses:
• The best choice for long-distance, all are solid, comfortable tourers.
• The many accessories will actually increase the value, but check that they all work.
• Very heavy bikes, and the standard brakes on Evo machines aren't really up to the weight.

2000 Road King:
100%

2000 Electra Glide Ultra Classic: **120%**

2000 Road Glide: **89%**

Softails

Softails are the Harleys with most retro appeal. Launched in 1984, they

The Fat Boy has been very successful – there are plenty around.

Even quite new bikes may be seriously customised.

The Evo-engined Dyna Glide is one of the most affordable bikes.

cleverly hide the rear shocks down by the swingarm, to give the appearance of a 1950s hardtail (hence the name) with a rigid rear end. An oil tank in its traditional place, plus external oil lines, complete the look, along with an engine bolted solidly into the frame without rubber mounts. Very early bikes also stuck with a four-speed gearbox and chain drive, while other Harleys went five-speed and belt drive.

From a practical point of view, the average Softail is inferior to an Electra Glide or Dyna. The hidden rear shocks have limited travel, and the rigidly mounted Evo engine transmits vibes to the rider – less of a problem with the balanced Twin Cam, though here the balance shafts sap power. There's limited luggage, and the riding position is uncomfortable beyond an hour, especially for pillions. But they do have that retro look that appeals to many, and make a good base for customising.

The first Softail was the FXST, based on a Wide Glide with 21-inch front wheel, four-speed, chain-drive, and even a kickstart as well as the electric starter. Two years later, it was updated to five-speed and belt drive, and joined by the Softail Custom with solid rear wheel, extra chrome and trim.

A bigger change was the Heritage Softail Special in '87, with fatter FL style shrouded forks and 16-inch front wheel. This led to the most successful Softail of all, the Fat Boy. Sixteen-inch solid disc wheels with fat tyres, shotgun exhausts and an all-over silver-grey finish. The Heritage Nostalgia (1991) added two-tone paint, whitewall tyres and special bags to the standard Heritage.

If the Heritage was retro, than the 1988 Springer was super-retro. For the first time since 1949, H-D ditched telescopic forks in favour of leading-link sprung forks, a modern replica of the type used from 1907. They were better than the originals, but inferior to any tele fork, stiffer and with shorter travel, while the skinny 21-inch front wheel limited braking power. But the Springer was so popular that it was, along with the Fat Boy, still part of the range over 20 years later. One early variant on the Springer Softail theme was the 1995 Bad Boy, with all-black finish.

Strengths/weaknesses:
• Retro appeal.
• Likely to have lower mileages than the touring bikes, and have been used for shorter jaunts on sunny days.
• Inferior comfort, handling and performance to other Big Twins.

Softail: **85%**
Softail Springer: **93%**
Heritage Softail Classic: **104%**
Fat Boy: **104%**

Twin Cam-engined Dyna Glide from 2005.

FX series/Dyna Glides

The FXR and Dyna Glide family arguably make the most practical road bikes of any Harley Big Twin. They're lighter than the FL's, have more comfort and better handling than the Softails, and are slightly quicker than both. On the downside, they aren't as distinctively Harleys as the other two families, at least in standard form. Tellingly, magazine testers loved these most rideable of Harleys, though they were outsold by the FLs and Softails.

The first of them was the FXR from 1984, with FLT-type rubber-mount frame (hence the nickname 'Rubber Glides') in a slimmer and more sporting package, with more ground clearance and twin front discs. It was soon joined by the Low Glide, with ultra-low seat and limited ground clearance, and FXRT, the latter a touring job with fairing and panniers. FXRDG was the Disc Glide, a limited addition with disc rear wheel and different paint.

All of these were five-speeds, and they gained belt drive in 1985. That same year, the new base model was the FXRS, available with a sport option of longer travel suspension and two front discs, while the Low Glide became the FXRC – that was 'C' for Custom, with stepped seat and high bars. The FXRT was also offered in police specification as the FXRP, all in white with full fairing and solo seat. Ex-police

FXRTs can be good buys, though of course they're difficult to find outside the US – higher mileage than usual, but well maintained and with a cache all of their own.

Other FXR variants were the Low Rider Custom from 1987, with 21in front wheel, and the Convertible from '89. The Convertible was so named because its screen and leather saddlebags were quickly detachable, making the bike adaptable to touring or summer cruising. Meanwhile, the sportiest Low Rider was the FXRS-SP, with low bars, longer suspension, and twin front discs. The FXRs were dropped in 1994. They had been gradually usurped by the Dyna Glides, which fulfilled exactly the same function within the Harley range, but had a slightly different frame. An improved rubber mounting system with fewer attachment points allowed Harley to hide the rear frame tubes. The forks were raked and wheelbase lengthened, which made the early Dyna Glides less sporty, and more cruiserish than the equivalent FXRs.

All pre-'06 Dynas were five-speed and belt drive, and the first bike to use the frame was the Sturgis for 1991. This revived a name used ten years earlier, and is a very collectible bike – it was only built for a year, so an original Sturgis, in black with cast wheels, is worth seeking out. The same applies to the Daytona that followed. Production models were the Dyna Glide Custom from 1992 and Wide Glide from '93, the latter with wide forks, spoked wheels (front 21in) and triple clamps.

For 1994, the basic Dyna chassis was sharpened up, with shorter fork rake and wheelbase plus longer suspension, which gave the bike more of the FXR's road manners. A Convertible was added, while the Low Rider and Wide Glide kept the old long wheelbase frame, though all Dynas got improved rubber mounts and forgings and castings for the frame junctions, instead of stampings. There were few major changes over the following years, the Dynas receiving the Twin Cam in 1999 and the six-speed gearbox in 2006, a year earlier than everything else.

Strengths/weaknesses:
• The rider's bike among the Big Twins – relatively good handling, comfort and performance.
• Cheaper to buy than the others.
• Less comfy for pillions (who should lobby for an Electra Glide).
• Doesn't have the style of tourers or Softails.
Dyna Super Glide: **72%**
Dyna Low Rider: **87%**
Dyna Wide Glide: **102%**
Dyna Super Glide Sport: **81%**
FXR Super Glide: **55%**
FXR Convertible: **63%**

The Fat Bob was a later Dyna Glide variant.

5 Before you view
– be well informed

To avoid a wasted journey, and the disappointment of finding that the bike does not match your expectations, it will help if you're very clear about what questions you want to ask before you pick up the phone. Some of these points might appear basic, but when you're excited about the prospect of buying your dream Harley, it's amazing how some of the most obvious things slip the mind ... Also check the current values of the model you are interested in in the classified ads.

Where is the bike?
Is it going to be worth travelling to the next county/state, or even across a border? A locally advertised machine, although it may not sound very interesting, can add to your knowledge for very little effort, so make a visit – it might even be in better condition than expected.

Dealer or private sale?
Establish early on if the bike is being sold by its owner or by a trader. A private owner should have all the history, so don't be afraid to ask detailed questions. A dealer may have more limited knowledge of the bike's history, but should have some documentation. A dealer may offer a warranty/guarantee (ask for a printed copy).

Cost of collection and delivery?
A dealer may well be used to quoting for delivery. A private owner may agree to meet you halfway, but only agree to this after you have seen the bike at the vendor's address to validate the documents. Conversely, you could meet halfway and agree the sale, but insist on meeting at the vendor's address for the handover.

View – when and where?
It is always preferable to view at the vendor's home or business premises. In the case of a private sale, the bike's documentation should tally with the vendor's name and address. Arrange to view only in daylight, and avoid a wet day – the vendor may be reluctant to let you take a test ride if it's wet.

Reason for sale?
Do make it one of the first questions. Why is the bike being sold and how long has it been with the current owner? How many previous owners?

Condition?
Ask for an honest appraisal of the bike's condition. Ask specifically about some of the check items described in chapter 8.

All original specification?
Very few Harleys remain completely standard, as many owners see the basic bike as a starting point for customising. So tracking down a 100 per cent original early Fat Boy, or Sturgis, or 90th Anniversary edition, amounts to quite a find. But unlike other bikes, accessories (especially H-D's own) can actually boost value rather than reduce it.

Matching data/legal ownership

Do frame, engine numbers and licence plate match the official registration document? Is the owner's name and address recorded in the official registration documents?

For those countries that require an annual test of roadworthiness, does the bike have a document showing it complies (an MoT certificate in the UK, which can be verified on 0845 600 5977)?

Does the bike carry a current road fund license/license plate tag? None of the Evo or Twin Cam Harleys qualify for historical vehicle road tax exempt status in the UK.

Does the vendor own the bike outright? Money might be owed to a finance company or bank: the bike could even be stolen. Several organisations will supply the data on ownership, based on the bike's licence plate number, for a fee. Such companies can often also tell you whether the bike has been 'written off' by an insurance company. In the UK these organisations can supply vehicle data:

HPI – 01722 422 422 – www.hpicheck.com
AA – 0870 600 0836 – www.theaa.com
RAC – 0870 533 3660 – www.rac.co.uk
Other countries will have similar organisations.

Insurance

Check with your existing insurer before setting out – your current policy might not cover you if you do buy the bike and decide to ride it home.

How you can pay

A cheque/check will take several days to clear and the seller may prefer to sell to a cash buyer. However, a banker's draft (a cheque issued by a bank) is as good as cash, but safer, so contact your own bank and become familiar with the formalities that are necessary to obtain one.

Buying at auction?

If the intention is to buy at auction see chapter 10 for further advice.

Professional vehicle check (mechanical examination)

In the UK, the AA and RAC no longer perform used motorcycle checks. A Harley dealer or independent specialist may be willing to check a bike over for a fee, but you'll need to get the owner's permission first.

6 Inspection equipment
– these items will really help

Before you rush out of the door, gather together a few items that will help as you work your way around the bike.

This book
This book is designed to be your guide at ever step, so take it along and use the check boxes in chapter 9 to help you assess each area of the bike. Don't be afraid to let the seller see you using it.

Reading glasses (if you need them for close work)
Taking your reading glasses if you need them to read documents and make close up inspections.

Overalls
Be prepared to get dirty. Take along a pair of overalls, if you have them.

Digital camera
A digital camera is handy so that later you can study some areas of the bike more closely. Take a picture of any part of the bike that causes you concern, and seek an expert opinion.

Compression tester
A compression tester is easy to use. It screws into the spark plug holes (and these are easy to get to on a Harley) and measures the compression as you spin the engine over on the starter. Remember to disconnect the other spark plug HT lead, to prevent the engine starting.

A friend, preferably a knowledgeable enthusiast
Ideally, have a friend or knowledgeable enthusiast come along with you to see the bike – a second opinion is always worth having.

7 Ten minute evaluation
– walk away or stay?

Documentation

If the seller claims to be the bike's owner, make sure he/she really is by checking the registration document, which in the UK is V5C. The person listed on the V5 isn't necessarily the legal owner, but their details should match those of whoever is selling the bike. Also use the V5C to check the engine/frame numbers.

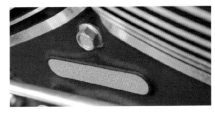

Engine/frame numbers reveal much.

An annual roadworthiness certificate – the 'MoT' in the UK – is not just handy proof that the bike was roadworthy when tested. A whole sheaf of them gives evidence of the bike's history – when it was actively being used, and what the mileage was. The more of these come with the bike, the better. Ask for any service history as well – routine servicing, repairs and recalls.

General condition

With the bike outside and in good light, take a good, slow walk around it. If it's claimed to be restored, and has a nice shiny tank and engine cases, look more closely – how far does the 'restored' finish go? Are the nooks and crannies behind the gearbox as spotless as the fuel tank? If not, the bike may have been given a quick smarten up to sell. A generally faded look all over isn't necessarily a bad thing – it suggests a machine that hasn't been restored, and isn't trying to pretend that it has.

Check the engine for leaks, nasty noises and smoke.

Now look at the engine – by far the most expensive and time consuming thing to put right if anything's wrong. There shouldn't be any oil leaks. Have a look at the front rubber mounting (on FLs, FXRs and Dynas) – if it's worn, it's a big job to replace.

Start the engine on the button – it should fire up promptly and rev up crisply and cleanly without showing blue or black smoke. Check that the oil light has gone out.

Check the drive belt for stone damage.

Listen for rumbles and knocks from the bottom end, and clonks from the primary drive – any of these are the precursors to serious work. While the engine's running, check that the ignition light has gone out – if it hasn't, the alternator isn't charging, though on Evos this could just be that the alternator/regular connector has pulled out.

Switch the engine off. Check for play in the forks, headstock and swingarm. Are there leaks from the front forks or rear shocks? You'll have to get down on the ground to examine the rear shocks on a Softail. And check the drive belt for stone damage.

How original is the bike? If you want a 100 per cent original machine, it could take some finding, as most Harley owners like to personalise the bike in some way. Bolt-on accessories can always be unbolted for a return to standard, but bikes that have undergone more major surgery may have reached the point of no return.

Spotting a fake
A few models are worth tracking down in original condition, as they are now rare and should make collectors' items in the future. The 1991 all-black Sturgis is a case in point, as is the very early FLT (which introduced rubber mountings) or the first Ultra Classic Electra Glide to offer fuel-injection. The first Fat Boys, if they've survived in their original silver/ grey paint with yellow highlights, are quite a find as well. Ditto a genuine police-spec FXRP, especially outside the US.

Paint and chrome work is important to any Harley.

The 90th Anniversary bikes and Liberty Editions are collectable too, if they've still got their original paint and graphics.

Of course, all of these are based on standard machines, so it's possible that what you're looking at may be a fake. Check the engine and frame numbers against the model codes in the back of this book to be sure. If the numbers on the engine and frame look as if they have been tampered with, walk away.

Are the bolt heads chewed or rounded off? Is there damage to casings around bolt heads? Has someone attacked fixings with a hammer and chisel? All are sure signs of a careless previous owner with more enthusiasm than skill, coupled with a dash of youthful impatience. Not a good sign.

Check engine and frame numbers against documentation – these will confirm who owns the bike, and whether it really is the model and year it's claiming to be.

Chrome is central to the look of just about every Harley Big Twin, so check it for tarnishing and rust.

Any oil leaks around the engine? They're rare, but can happen and are a hassle to fix.

Check for evidence of crash damage, on crashbars if they're fitted, and on footboards, forks, silencers, and luggage if they're not.

Score each section using the boxes as follows:
4 = excellent; 3 = good; 2 = average; 1 = poor. The totting up procedure is detailed at the end of the chapter. Be realistic in your marking!

Engine/frame numbers

The last six digits of the engine number should match those of the frame number.

The bike's VIN – Vehicle Identification Number – is crucial for two reasons. Matching it to the documentation is evidence that the bike is not stolen, and it can tell you a lot about the machine you are looking it, including the exact model. That's especially useful if someone is trying to pass off, say, a standard FXRT as a rare, police-spec CHP version.

The full VIN is on the frame, on the right-hand side of the headstock on most bikes, and slightly further back on that side on FLs. Engine numbers are all on the left-hand side on top of the crankcase, and it's easy to check that the frame is carrying its original engine, as both share the same numbers, which are the last six digits of each.

If these six digits don't match, then the bike will have had an engine swap at some point. That doesn't necessarily mean it's not worth buying, but you need to ask the seller why this happened. The result could be a perfectly good, legitimate

The frame VIN can tell you a lot.

The VIN is also on a plate on the frame downtube.

motorcycle, but the price should reflect the fact that it isn't original.

Let's take a fictitious VIN of 1 HD 1 BPK 12 YY 123456. '1' means made in USA ('5' is Canada); 'HD' stands for the make and the second '1' is the class of bike (over 900cc). 'BP' is the model code, which in this case refers to a Bad Boy. 'YY' is the model year (2000 in this

The VIN is stamped onto the frame.

case) – Evo-engined bikes use a letter, Twin Cams a number. From 2001, the letter after the model code showed which factory the bike was built in – in this case, 'K' for Kansas City.

If the frame or engine number looks as if it has been tampered with, or if the numbers don't match the documentation, and the seller doesn't have a convincing explanation as to why this is the case, walk away – there are plenty of used Harleys on the market with straight, honest histories.

Paint   4 3 2 1

Paintwork plays a massive part of any Harley's appeal, and for the most part owners take pride in appearances, so expect the paint to be pretty good. Anything shabby is a good bargaining point to reduce the asking price.

Harley paint is generally good quality, but the lacquer that protects it is relatively soft and easily scratched, especially in black. Minor scratches will polish out quite easily and again, a conscientious owner will keep on top of this. Check the paintwork around the pillion footrests, especially on tourers – this can get scuffed as pillions climb on and off the bike.

If the paint looks a real mess, with peeling lacquer, it's likely that water has got in through a crack in the lacquer

Paintwork is expensive to put right.

and spread underneath it, causing it to peel and dissolve. The answer is to strip the lacquer off and polish the paintwork underneath.

If looking at a custom paint job, think carefully, especially if it involves painstakingly airbrushed murals. Is it something you can live with (half-naked she-devils aren't to everyone's taste) and if it does get scratched, restoring it will be an expensive and time-consuming job. On the other hand, if the bike has its original paint, then that's a positive bonus, as many bikes do get repainted over the years, often in a shade or design of the owner's choosing. Find a 1991 Sturgis, or one of the Anniversary Editions (such as the 90th in 1993, or the Liberty) with its paintwork and graphics intact and in good condition, and that will add to the value.

Chrome

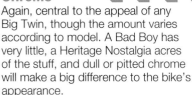

Again, central to the appeal of any Big Twin, though the amount varies according to model. A Bad Boy has very little, a Heritage Nostalgia acres of the stuff, and dull or pitted chrome will make a big difference to the bike's appearance.

This chrome is perfect.

The good news is that Harley-Davidson (as you'd expect) is good at chrome, and it is decent quality to start with. Actually, the 1980s and '90s Evo-engined bikes are thought to have better quality plating than the Twin Cams. This was down to new restrictions on the plating process, which banned some hazardous chemicals – good for the plating workers, but it means that Twin Cam chrome does need more looking after.

So check all the chrome parts for rust, pitting and general dullness. Minor blemishes can be polished away, but otherwise you're looking at a replating bill. If the silencers are seriously rotted, it's a better idea to budget for a new pair – less hassle than getting the old ones replated in any case. And items like a chrome oil tank will involve extra workshop hours in removing/replacing them, as well as the plating bill itself.

Even if the bike has perfect chrome, the bottom line is that you will need to work hard to keep it that way.

Cared-for chrome is part of a Harley's appeal.

Unplated alloy can become dull, too.

Bodywork

In one respect, buying a secondhand bike is easier than purchasing a used car – there's far less bodywork to worry about. And for Harley Big Twins, as with paint, the amount varies according to model – very little on a basic Dyna Glide, plenty on a fully dressed Road Glide.

Whichever bike you're looking at, the fuel tank needs to be checked for leaks

There's more bodywork on the tourers – this is an Electra Glide leg shield.

around the tap (on carburettor models) and along the seams, as well as dents and rust. Watch out for patches of filler. Repairing leaks means flushing the tank out (which has to be thorough – you don't want any petrol vapour hanging about when the welding torch is fired up), but the fuel tank is at least easy to remove. Pinhole leaks can often be cured by Petseal, but anything more serious needs a proper repair. If the tank is beyond saving, new ones

Check crashbars for evidence of ... a crash.

are available, though once it's been painted, that's not a cheap option. So a very poor condition tank is a good bargaining lever. The oil tank, in its traditional position on Softails, is well protected, so that shouldn't be a problem.

Mudguards, too, should be straight, free of rust around the rims, and securely bolted to the bike. Also check the fork shrouds on FLs and the Fat Boy, as these are vulnerable to damage. On early Fat Boys, the shrouds can actually hit the mudguard under heavy braking. A recall in 2006 replaced the shrouds with new items that included a semicircular cutout on the inside to clear the mudguard. On pre-'06 bikes, check that this has been done.

On the Electra Glide, Road Glide, and Street Glide (and in fact anything with hard panniers) the fairing, panniers, and top box, plus several other bodywork parts such as fairing lowers and rear

Glassfibre should be free of cracks.

covers are made of fibreglass. Again, it's good quality stuff that shouldn't give any trouble, but it does need to be checked for cracks and crazing – the latter could just be the paint, but serious cracking really means replacing the whole part, as seamless repairs are a tricky business.

While looking around the bodywork, keep an eye out for evidence of crash damage, especially on the crash bars (if fitted) and footpegs or boards. We're not talking high speed collisions here, but low speed (or even stationary!) toppling over which on bikes as heavy as this can inflict a lot of damage.

Badges/transfers ☑ ☑ ☑ ☑

Are the bike's original badges and/or transfers in place? There have been such a multiplicity of these over the years that getting hold of replacements

Original badges are a bonus.

Badges and graphics often evoke an earlier era – the 1930s, in this case.

could be a problem. Not that this bothers many owners, who would rather personalise the bike in any case.

Seat ☑ ☑ ☑ ☑

Whichever seat a Harley has – and they do vary a great deal according to model – the points to look for are the same. Metal pans can rust, which will eventually give way, though this is easy to check. Covers can split, which of course allows rain in, which the foam padding soaks up ... and never dries out. That's a recipe for a permanently wet backside, or a rock hard seat on frosty mornings (the author speaks from experience). New covers and complete seats in

Check seat for splits and tears – this one is pristine.

various styles are available, though recovering an old seat is a specialist job.

As Harleys are easy bikes to customise, there's a big choice of seats available, whether from H-D itself or aftermarket suppliers, which will bolt straight on. So if the seat does need refurbishing, it could be a good opportunity to replace a solo seat with a dual, or vice versa.

Don't forget the pillion perch as well.

Rubbers

Worn footrest/footboard rubbers are a good sign of high mileage, though as they're so cheap and easy to replace, not an infallible one. They should be secure on the footrest and free of splits or tears. If the footrest itself is bent upwards, that's a sure sign the bike has been down the road at some point, so look for other telltale signs on that side. The kickstart (where fitted) and gearchange rubbers are also easy to replace, so well worn ones could indicate owner neglect.

Worn rubbers indicate mileage – these are hardly used.

Footrest rubbers should be secure.

Frame

The three families of Big Twin use different frames, though even these are strongly related. The Softail frame, for example, with its hidden rear shocks, was an adaption of the old Superglide frame. The anti-vibration rubber-mount frame of the FLT and Electra Glide was adapted for use in the FXR, which in turn was modified to form the basis of the Dyna Glide.

The most important job is to check whether the main frame is straight and true. Crash damage may have bent it,

Serious frame misalignment should show up on the test ride.

Softail rear frame.

Check steering head area for evidence of a front end collision.

putting the wheels out of line. One way of checking is with an experienced eye, string, and a straight edge, but the surest way to ascertain a frame's straightness is on the test ride – any serious misalignment should be obvious in the way the bike handles. If it pulls to one side, or weaves in a straight line, a bent frame is one of a number of possible causes, and needs further investigation before you commit yourself. If the bike doesn't feel right, look for other evidence of crash damage – not just the obvious, but suspiciously new parts on an otherwise old bike. Why would someone fit a complete set of new forks, or replace just one mirror?

The frame's cosmetics aren't so obvious as those of the bodywork, but easily overlooked, as it's simply easier to repaint tank and mudguards. A frame that is really shabby necessitates a strip down and repaint, though as with the other paintwork, if it's original and fits in with the patina of the bike, then there's a good case for leaving it as it is. Finally, check that any brackets on the frame are in one piece.

The side stand is strong, but check it doesn't wobble.

Side stand ④ ③ ② ①

Harleys don't have centre stands (which causes a problem in itself – see below) so depend on a substantial side stand to prop up the whole bike when parked. Fortunately, it really is substantial, well up to coping with the bike's weight, so it's unlikely to need attention unless the bike has been very well used and/ or a portly owner has made a habit of sitting on the bike while it's supported by the stand. Some Harley stands have a disconcerting tendency of allowing the bike to slip forward an inch or two, as if it's not actually locked in place, but this is nothing to worry about.

Don't forget the spotlights on Electra Glides and Road Kings.

Rear/stop light failure is usually just the bulb.

Lights

Harleys of this era have good lights, backed up by reliable electrics, so they shouldn't be a problem, but check that they work, whether on permanently (on later bikes in some markets) or via the switch. Don't forget to check the riding lights on Electra Glides and Road Kings – these aren't designed to be left on permanently, but some riders do that, and bulbs can fail. Still, nothing makes drivers notice an approaching bike more than headlight plus twin riding lights blazing!

All electrical connections (coil to plugs here) should be tight.

Electrics/wiring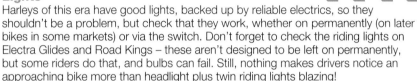

Old Harleys, like British and Italian machines from a past era, had a reputation for poor electrics, but this was largely banished during the Evo era. However, the electrical system still needs checking. A good general indication of the owner's attitude is the condition of the wiring – is it tidy and neat, or flopping around? That's especially the case where aftermarket riding lights or indicators have been fitted by an owner – the neatness of the wiring says a lot about their ability. The many connectors need to be clean and tight, and many odd electrical problems are simply down to bad connections or a poor earth.

Regulators on Evos are prone to burning out, and if this happens on a closed circuit it simply flattens battery. If it happens on an open circuit, it burns the battery out and can damage the alternator stator as well. Fortunately, it's

Accessory plugs on fully dressed bikes need checking, too.

simple to check – if the charge light goes off when the engine is running, then all is well. Also on Evos, the regulator bullet connector can pop out, so lack of charging could be just this – check this just behind the rear rubber mounting if the battery isn't charging.

Finally, check that everything electrical works: lights, horn, starter, indicators, and stop light, plus any sound system.

Wheels/tyres

On spoked wheels check the chrome condition on the rims (unless they happen to be alloy rims of course) – rechroming entails a complete dismantle and rebuild of the wheel. Check that none of the spokes are loose and give each one a gentle tap with a screwdriver – any that are 'off-key' will need retensioning. Alloy wheels should be checked for cracks, though there's no evidence that Harley's alloy wheels are prone to this.

Tyres should be to at least the legal minimum. In the UK, that's at least 1mm of tread depth across at least three-quarters of the breadth of the tyre. Or if the tread doesn't reach that far across the breadth (true of some modern tyres) then any tread showing

Tap the spokes – a loose one will sound off-key.

Tread depth and general damage is what to look for here.

must be at least 1mm deep. Beware of bikes that have been left standing for some time, allowing the tyres to crack and deterioriate – it's no reason to reject the bike, but a good lever to reduce the price. Most tyre sizes are available from a choice of manufacturers, and they won't break the bank, unless a previous owner has fitted an oversize rear rim and ultra-fat tyre to match.

Wheel bearings

Wheel bearings aren't expensive, but fitting them is a hassle, and if there's play it could affect the handling. They are less likely to need attention on post-2000 bikes, which had sealed bearings that don't need greasing. The usual method of checking is to put the bike on its centre stand so that either wheel is off the ground, but you can't do that with a Harley. The only reliable answer is to take a paddock stand or small

Wheel bearings are tricky to check without a paddock stand ...

... but the rear wheel is easier than the front.

car jack and lift each end of the bike up in turn – a few inches will do it, but take care where the jack is located. Have a helper steady the bike as you do this, and while you are checking the bearings. Put the steering on full lock and try rocking the front wheel in a vertical plane, then spin the wheel and listen for signs of roughness. Do the same for the rear wheel. But don't be too worried if you don't have a jack or paddock stand, and this all seems like too much hassle – if the bike handles well and the bearings are quiet then they're probably OK.

Steering head bearings
Again, the bearings don't cost and arm or leg, but trouble here can affect the handling, and changing them is a big job. With the bike on that jack or paddock stand, swing the handlebars from lock to lock. They should move freely, with not a hint of roughness or stiff patches – if there is, budget for replacing them. To check for play, put the steering on full lock, grip the front wheel and try rocking it back and forth. With the front wheel on the ground, apply the front brake and try to push bike forward – there should be no clonks, though this can be confused with fork wear (see below).

Swing arm bearings
Another essential for good handling is the swing arm bearings. To check for wear, get hold of the rear end of the arm on one side and try rocking the complete

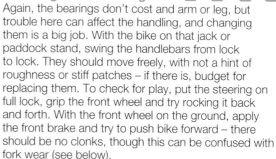

Steering head bearings live here, just below the bars.

The swingarm is easy to find on FXR/Dynas.

swing arm from side to side. There should be no perceptible movement. This check is only really possible on the FXR and Dyna Glide – the Softail rear end doesn't use a conventional swing arm, and the arm is very difficult to get to on luggage-equipped FLs.

Forks should be free of leaks – the FL's shrouding helps protect them.

Suspension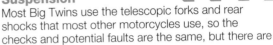

Most Big Twins use the telescopic forks and rear shocks that most other motorcycles use, so the checks and potential faults are the same, but there are a couple of Harley-only features you won't find anywhere else.

Taking the conventional side first, examine the forks for oil leaks, and the stanchions for rust and pitting. The stanchions aren't visible on the shrouded forks of the FLs, Fat Boy and others, but these are at least protected from the weather. Check for wear in the fork bushes by holding the front brake on and pumping the forks up and down – there should be no clonks or feeling of looseness. Another method is to hold the front wheel on full lock, and attempt to move the bars.

Rear shocks should be examined for leaks as well (though you'll have trouble seeing them on a Softail, or any bike with hard panniers) but the

Springer fork problems are down to tight or loose bushes.

real check of how worn out they are comes on the test ride. If the rear end is bouncing without much apparent damping control, then the shocks are badly worn.

Now for the oddities. Springer forks rely for their integrity on numerous teflon bearings, and if these are set too loose or tight, then handling will suffer. They are adjustable, and according to the service schedule

One way of checking for fork and steering head bearing play.

Also check rear shocks for leaks, if you can see them.

generally need setting up every 10,000 miles. Don't forget to check the single shock in the Springer system for leaks.

Some FLs have air-assisted suspension, which allows quick and easy adjustment of spring rates. Adjustment is via a Schrader valve, on the left-hand side of the bars on early bikes, and next to the left-hand pannier on later ones. Connection hoses (which were just a push-fit) can pop off on early bikes – later hoses were more secure. If hoses do come adrift the suspension still works, but check that all they are in place.

Later speedos are electronic, not cable-driven. Note the fuel gauge in the dummy tank cap.

Tank-mounted speedo and rev counter on a Dyna Glide.

Electra Glides tell you everything you could possibly want to know!

Instruments

Instrumentation ranges from a single tank-mounted speedo to a full set of dials on the Electra and Road Glides. Either way, check on the test ride that all are functioning. All speedometers were electronic from 1995, so any faults from that date are likely to be poor contacts. Pre-'95, if both speedo and mileometer aren't working, the cable to both is the most likely fault. If one or the other is dead, then evidence points to the relevant mechanism.

Have a good look around the engine. This is a Twin Cam.

Engine/gearbox – general impression

You can tell a lot about the likely condition of a Harley V-twin without hearing it run. These engines are relatively easy to work on, which can encourage keen and/ or impecunious owners to take things apart themselves, sometimes without the proper tools. So look for chewed screw or allen bolt heads, and rounded off bolts, plus damage to the casings surrounding them.

The Evolution engine famously put an end to Harley's reputation for oil leaks, but they can still happen. Evos can leak from the cylinder base gasket, partly due to the routing of an oil drain passage. 1991-92 bikes were worst affected, but a metal gasket (which can be retro-fitted) was a big improvement, and the problem was all but

Six-speed gearbox from 2007 gives very relaxed cruising.

Front rubber mounting lives behind here.

Oil leaks are unlikely, but check anyway.

eliminated by 1998. Also check the timing cover for leaks. Twin Cams can leak at sustained high speeds, when oil accumulates in the rocker boxes, and some aftermarket 95in^3 kits can cause excess oil venting. The CVO110 (and some TC96s) can leak from just below the exhaust port on the rear cylinder. But generally, oil leaks are a thing of the past, thanks to tighter tolerances and better gaskets – they're very rare.

Check the engine oil – correct level? Nice and clean? Look for traces of the telltale 'mayonnaise' that indicates a lot of short journeys. Many of the same comments apply to the gearbox – look for chewed fasteners and signs of neglect. Remove the oil filler cap and stick a finger inside to check whether the oil had been changed recently – nice clean EP90 ... or a frothy sludge?

Is the engine standard, or has it been tuned? A stage 1 kit is very common, and many owners fit big-capacity kits to boost performance. The golden rule with any tuning is, who did it, and did they do a proper job? These are strong engines that can run to 100,000 miles if looked after, but radical or badly carried out tuning can shorten their life dramatically.

All Evo and Twin Cams, except the Softails, have the engine rubber mounted to quell vibration. The rubbers rarely give trouble, but should be checked every 10,000 miles, and it's certainly worth looking at the front mount. This has to cope with all acceleration and braking forces, and is the first mount to break down – listen for rattles here, which are a sign of wear.

Engine – starting/idling

Start the engine. It should fire up promptly whether cold or hot and settle down to a slow, reliable idle. Does the starter motor engage cleanly? If the motor's reluctant to fire, there could be one of a number of causes, though the electronic ignition, carburettor and injection systems are all pretty reliable. On carburettor bikes, a lumpy, uneven idle is probably just down to adjustment, but any possible injection problems will involve a trip to the dealer. Carb Harleys only have one carburettor, not two (or four) that have to be synchronised.

The engine should start promptly on the button.

If the bike you're looking at is being started for the first time after a long lay-up (eg over winter), then beware. On Evos, the gravity feed oil tank allows oil to drain into the crankcase over time, so at first start-up the oil pump scavanges this excess out of the vent pipe. It's not a sign of major problems, but messy and alarming when it happens. So to be sure, check the oil level before starting up – if it's very low, then 'wet sumping,' as this is called, is likely to be the cause. Twin Cam Dynas and FLs don't suffer from this, because their oil tank is mounted low. Twin Cam Softails still have a gravity tank, but by 2000 Harley had managed to overcome the oil drain problem.

Engine – smoke/noise

With the engine warm, blip the throttle and watch for smoke. White smoke is harmless, just water vapour escaping as the engine warms up. Black smoke is due to an over-rich mixture, the most likely cause on carburettor bikes (apart from a blocked air filter) being a wrongly jetted carb to suit an aftermarket air cleaner and/or exhaust. Even a stage 1 kit will need the carb or injection set up to suit afterwards. Blue smoke is more serious – the engine is burning oil, which is down to straightforward wear at the top end. You're unlikely to come across this unless the engine has covered 40,000 miles or more.

Listen to the engine. A lot of people think of Harleys as naturally noisy, but hydraulic tappets and lots of attention to noise reduction have made them fairly quiet mechnically. Loud pipes are there because the owner likes the noise they make – they're not compulsory. Listen for knocks and rumbles from the bottom end, but again, this is unlikely unless the bike is very high mileage or oil changes have been neglected.

Not a Harley, but blue smoke will look like this.

Some mechanical problems can't be detected. On very early Twin Cams (1999/early 2000) the rear cam bearings can disintegrate, but a change from ball to roller bearings in late 2000 solved this. Pre-'06 Twin Cams used a spring-loaded cam chain tensioner that could wear rapidly as the 'silent' cam chain's sharp edges bit into it. This is potentially serious, as the tensioner pad breaks up, sending particles around the engine. Some bikes simply aren't affected by either problem, but it's worth a look at the service history to see if it has suffered in the past. 2006-on bikes had an hydraulic tensioner and roller chain, which solved the problem.

Primary drive

④ ③ ② ①

Listen to the primary drive while the engine is running. Noises from this area – clonks or rumbles – could be one of a number of things. It could be wear in the clutch and its shock absorber, or the engine sprocket chattering on worn splines. Of course, you won't know which without taking the primary drive cover off, but if the seller acknowledges that a noise is there, it's another good lever to reduce the price.

All Big Twins have a primary chain, and on the Evo this is manually adjusted, a job easily overlooked as the adjuster is out of sight. If the chain is allowed to run slack it will eventually start to flap around and even start gouging its way into the case. Listen for rattles from the left-hand side – they should be obvious when the engine is started. This isn't a problem on Twin Cams, with their automatic hydraulic chain adjuster.

Listen for rattles and rumbles from primary drive.

Belt/sprockets ④ ③ ② ①

Some early Evos – 1984/85 – stuck with chain drive, but every Big Twin since has used Harley's toothed belt to drive the rear wheel. This is good news, because the belts have a life of 60,000 miles and don't need lubing, nor should they need tensioning between tyre changes. There's actually no official change interval, but the belt's life can be as little as 30,000 miles if the bike is radically tuned.

Have an assistant push the bike forward to check the entire belt.

What is more likely to end a belt's life is small stones getting trapped between belt and sprocket – these can actually punch a hole in the belt, which will eventually snap. To check, have an assistant slowly push the bike forwards while you make a visual check of the belt – any damage should be obvious. The bike is actually still rideable (on a go easy, get-you-home basis) with damage to the centre of the belt, but any damage to the side will soon cause the belt to snap. Also check the sprocket teeth, which get rougher as they wear, which in turn wears the belt more rapidly.

If the belt needs replacing, expect to pay £500 for a dealer to do the job. It'll cost more if the sprockets need replacing as well; ditto if the bike is an early FXR, which needs the swingarm to be removed before the old belt can come off.

Rust can attack internals, especially if the bike has been used for short trips.

These are standard silencers – often they'll be aftermarket items.

Exhaust

Any serious corrosion should be obvious on the exhaust (though Dynas have a well hidden balance pipe), but to check for leaks, hold a rag over the end of each pipe in turn while the engine is running. If there's a chuffing sound, you have a leak somewhere on that pipe, but if the engine faulters or dies, then all is well. If there is a problem, it could just be a leaky gasket, rather than something that requires a complete new system.

Luggage

Many Harleys have luggage. On hard panniers and topboxes, check that the locks work and that there's no sign of water ingress inside. On the outside, look for cracks, crazing or signs of crash damage. Softails often come with

Leather saddlebags reinforce the image of a 'high plains drifter.'

Hard panniers are more waterproof, and lockable.

Check that the panniers and topbox are dry inside.

leather panniers, which aren't water- or thief-proof but do look the part. Staining indicates they've been left out in the rain, and look for scuffs on the leather.

A screen is a popular accessory, and standard on some bikes.

Accessories   ①

Unlike most bikes, accessories can actually increase the value of a secondhand Harley. That's as long as they're genuine Harley or quality aftermarket parts, preferably dealer fitted. Ask the owner who fitted the accessories, and look out for DIY wiring jobs.

The bike is very likely to have a non-standard exhaust (whether Screamin' Eagle or from an independent) – free-flowing air filter, Dynojet (on carb bikes) and Power Commander (on injecteds) are also common. In each case, check that the bike runs cleanly on the test ride – if it doesn't, it hasn't been set up properly.

Loud pipes are less common than they used to be, as noise regulations get tighter around the world, and more strictly enforced. In the UK, riders were often let off with a verbal warning, but now a fine and licence points are more common. If the pipes are marked 'off-road use only' then they are not road legal.

Security ④ ③ ② ①

It's a sad fact of life that Harleys are extremely stealable, because there are lots of them about (so it's easier to pass one off as another), they hold their value well, and are in high demand. So use those documentation and engine/frame number checks to be as sure as you can that the bike is legitimate. 2002-06 bikes had remote immobilisers, and from 2006 on have proximity ignition keys. These are harder to replace than standard keys, so check that the bike has its spare.

Test ride

The test ride should be no less than 15 minutes, and you should be doing the riding – not the seller riding with you on the pillion. It's understandable that some sellers are reluctant to let a complete stranger loose on their pride and joy, but it does go with the territory of selling a bike, and so long as you leave an article of faith (usually the vehicle you arrived in) then all should be happy. Take your driving licence in case the seller wants to see it.

Main warning lights

The warning light array and location varies according to model – pictured is the warning light cluster on an Evo Dyna Glide. Check that ignition, oil, and (if fitted) fuel-injection and ABS warning lights go off when the bike is started and/or moving.

The oil light (second from right) should go out once the engine starts.

Engine performance

Standard Big Twins don't have a lot of power, but what they do have is torque in abundance, so these bike aren't quite as slow as some people would have you believe. Wind the throttle open, even from low speeds, and the bike should surge forward regardless of which gear it's in (except maybe the high sixth of late Twin Cams). Acceleration should be strong up to 60-70mph, where aerodynamics start to take over.

Carburettor bikes sometimes suffer from hesitation at around 3000rpm, but the injecteds should give

The V-twins deliver good, torquey performance when all is well.

seamless torque right through the rev range. If they or the carb bikes do hesitate and hiccup, then it's likely to be down to tuning parts, bolted on without the bike being set up properly afterwards.

Back from the test ride, and with the engine hot, it should settle down to a steady, even idle. Don't be alarmed by the heat billowing up from the engine on a hot day – Twin Cams do this more, because they're better able to dissipate heat, thanks to more generous finning.

On the test ride, the engine should have good throttle response and a strong mid-range.

Clutch operation ☐4 ☐3 ☐2 ☐1

The clutch is heavier than on some other modern bikes, but it won't need a Charles Atlas hand to operate it, and take up should be smooth and positive. Nor should it drag or slip. To check this, select first gear from a standstill. A small crunch is normal, but a full-blooded graunch, followed by a leap forward, means the clutch is dragging. However, the cure is usually down to careful adjustment rather than the wholesale replacement of parts.

The clutch should be smooth and progressive.

Gearbox operation ☐4 ☐3 ☐2 ☐1

If you're used to the 'electric switch' type gear change of other bikes, the Harley may come as a shock. The change is long travel and deliberate, needing a firm, positive foot. That's not necessarily a bad thing, and for some it's part of the bike's appeal. The six-speed is better, though some early examples suffer from a noisy fifth gear, especially in hot weather. Whatever the gearbox, listen for excessive whining and watch for it jumping out of gear.

Some bikes have a heel-toe gearchange.

Handling ☐4 ☐3 ☐2 ☐1

Again, you shouldn't expect a Harley to handle like a Japanese sports tourer, but they do go round corners better than you might think. The biggest limitation is ground clearance, especially on Softails, tourers and certain FXR/Dynas. Take that into account, and the Big Twins handle quite well. There shouldn't be any vagueness in a straight line, but expect some wallowing in corners – handling problems can be down to something as simple as incorrect tyre pressures or badly worn tyres. Otherwise, it could be worn forks or shocks, or wheel, steering head or swing arm bearings. If you do get a chance to test ride a new Harley at a dealer first, then take the opportunity – it'll give you an idea of how things should be.

Later brakes, with four-pot calipers, are a big improvement.

Brakes

Evo brakes have become almost a byword in mediocrity, and there's no getting away from the fact that the single front and rear discs with two-pot calipers need a really hard squeeze to stop a 300kg bike at speed. That's why many riders fit aftermarket four- or even six-pot calipers, which do a good job. Harris is a favourite and very good quality, also a sign of a previous owner willing to spend serious money on the bike. The standard brakes aren't dangerous, but upgraded calipers are well worthwhile.

Happily, Twin Cam brakes are far better, with four-pot calipers on the front to give 21st century stopping power. Whichever bike you're looking at, check the discs for scores and wear lips – the minimum thickness should be stamped at the centre of the disc. ABS became an option on all tourers in 2008, and standard on the CVO 110. If fitted, check that the warning light goes off once the bike gets moving – it flashes on start up, but this is a normal diagnostic check.

Dragging brakes indicate sticking calipers.

Check the pads and discs for wear.

The master cylinder shouldn't be leaky.

Cables

The control cables – clutch, throttle, and (on carburettor bikes) choke – should work smoothly without stiffness or jerking. Poorly lubricated, badly adjusted cables are an indication of general neglect, and the same goes for badly routed cables. 2008-on tourers have a fly by wire electronic throttle, which doesn't use a cable.

The clutch cable (plus throttle and choke, if fitted) should work smoothly.

Switchgear

Switchgear is straightforward and generally reliable, with no particular faults. But check that everything works, especially on fully-loaded tourers with a bewildering array of switches.

The switchgear is reliable.

Don't forget accessory switchgear.

Sidecars

Almost unique among modern manufacturers, Harley has offered both trikes and sidecar outfits from the factory. The sidecar was reintroduced in 1991, but few were made and they are very rare. You're more likely to come across a bike that has been fitted with an aftermarket sidecar, such as Watsonian in the UK. If looking at any outfit, and if you haven't used a sidecar before, think carefully. They demand a completely different riding technique to a solo, pulling one side on acceleration, the other on braking is normal (for a UK spec LH chair). Check that the outfit doesn't wander in a straight line and that all mountings are tight and secure. In 2009, Harley introduced the Tri-Glide, a factory-built trike that really takes off where the sidecar outfit stops.

Evaluation procedure

Add up the total points.
Score: 144 = excellent; 108 = good; 72 = average; 36 = poor.
Bikes scoring over 101 will be completely usable and will require only maintenance and care to preserve condition. Bikes scoring between 36 and 73 will require some serious work (at much the same cost regardless of score). Bikes scoring between 74 and 107 will require very careful assessment of the necessary repair/restoration costs in order to arrive at a realistic value.

10 Auctions
– sold! Another way to buy your dream

Auction pros & cons
Pros: Prices will usually be lower than those of dealers or private sellers, and you might grab a real bargain on the day. Auctioneers have usually established clear title with the seller. At the venue you can usually examine documentation relating to the vehicle.
Cons: You have to rely on a sketchy catalogue description of condition and history. The opportunity to inspect is limited, and you cannot ride the bike. Auction bikes are often a little below par and may require some work. It's easy to overbid. There will usually be a buyer's premium to pay in addition to the auction hammer price.

Which auction?
Auctions by established auctioneers are advertised in bike magazines and on the auction houses' websites. A catalogue, or a simple printed list of the lots for auction, might only be available a day or two ahead, though often lots are listed and pictured on auctioneers' websites much earlier. Contact the auction company to ask if previous auction selling prices are available as this is useful information (details of past sales are often available on websites).

Catalogue, entry fee, and payment details
When you purchase the catalogue of the vehicles in the auction, it often acts as a ticket allowing two people to attend the viewing days and the auction. Catalogue details tend to be comparatively brief, but will include information such as 'one owner from new, low mileage, full service history', etc. It will also usually show a guide price to give you some idea of what to expect to pay, and will tell you what is charged as a 'Buyer's premium.' The catalogue will also contain details of acceptable forms of payment. At the fall of the hammer an immediate deposit is usually required, the balance payable within 24 hours. If you plan to pay by cash note that there may be a cash limit. Some auctions will accept payment by debit card; and sometimes credit or charge cards are acceptable, but will often incur an extra charge. A bank draft or bank transfer will have to be arranged in advance with your own bank as well as with the auction house. No bike will be released before all payments are cleared. If delays occur in payment transfers then storage costs can accrue.

Buyer's premium
A buyer's premium will be added to the hammer price: don't forget this in your calculations. It is not usual for there to be a further state tax or local tax on the purchase price and/or on the buyer's premium.

Viewing
In some instances it's possible to view on the day, or days, before, as well as in the hours prior to the auction. Auction officials may be willing to help out by opening engine and luggage compartments and may allow you to inspect the interior. While the officials may start the engine for you, a test ride is out of the question. Crawling

under and around the bike as much as you want is permitted. You can also ask to see any documentation available.

Bidding

Before you take part in the auction, decide on your maximum bid – and stick to it!

It may take a while for the auctioneer to reach the lot you're interested in, so use that time to observe how other bidders behave. When it's the turn of your bike, attract the auctioneer's attention and make an early bid. The auctioneer will then look to you for a reaction every time another bid is made; usually the bids will be in fixed increments until the bidding slows, whereupon smaller increments will often be accepted before the hammer falls. If you want to withdraw from the bidding, make sure the auctioneer understands your intentions – a vigorous shake of the head when he or she looks to you for the next bid should do the trick!

Assuming that you are the successful bidder, the auctioneer will note your card or paddle number, and from that moment on you will be responsible for the vehicle.

If the bike is unsold, either because it failed to reach the reserve or because there was little interest, it may be possible to negotiate with the owner, via the auctioneer, after the sale is over.

Successful bid

There are two more items to think about: how to get the bike home; and insurance. If you can't ride the bike, your own or a hired trailer is one way, another is to have the vehicle shipped using the facilities of a local company. The auction house will also have details of companies specialising in the transfer of bikes.

Insurance for immediate cover can usually be purchased on site, but it may be more cost-effective to make arrangements with your own insurance company in advance, and then call to confirm the full details.

eBay & other online auctions

eBay and other online auctions could land you a bike at a bargain price, though you'd be foolhardy to bid without examining the bike first, something most vendors encourage. A useful feature of eBay is that the geographical location of the bike is shown, so you can narrow your choices to those within a realistic radius of home. Be prepared to be outbid in the last few moments of the auction. Remember, your bid is binding, and it will be very, very difficult to get restitution in the case of a crooked vendor fleecing you – caveat emptor!

Be aware that some bikes offered for sale in online auctions are 'ghost' bikes. Don't part with any cash without being sure that the vehicle does actually exist and is as described (usually pre-bidding inspection is possible).

Auctioneers

Barrett-Jackson www.barrett-jackson.com
Bonhams www.bonhams.com
British Car Auctions (BCA) www.bca-europe.com or www.british-car-auctions.co.uk
Cheffins www.cheffins.co.uk
Christies www.christies.com
Coys www.coys.co.uk
Dorset Vintage and Classic Auctions www.dvca.co.uk
eBay www.ebay.com
H&H www.classic-auctions.co.uk
RM www.rmauctions.com
Shannons www.shannons.com.au
Silver www.silverauctions.com

11 Paperwork
– correct documentation is essential!

The paper trail

Pre-owned bikes come with a large portfolio of paperwork accumulated and passed on by a succession of proud owners. This documentation represents the real history of the bike, and from it can be deduced the level of care the bike has received, how much it's been used, which specialists have worked on it, and the dates of major repairs and restorations. All of this information will be priceless to you as the new owner, so be very wary of bikes with little or no paperwork to support their claimed history.

Registration documents

All countries/states have some form of registration for private vehicles, whether it's like the American 'pink slip' system or the British 'log book' systems.

It's essential to check that the registration document is genuine, that it relates to the bike in question, and that all the vehicle's details are correctly recorded, including frame and engine numbers (if these are shown). If you are buying from the previous owner, his or her name and address will be recorded in the document: this will not be the case if you're buying from a dealer.

In the UK, the current (Euro-aligned) registration document is named 'V5C,' and is printed in coloured sections of blue, green and pink. The blue section relates to the motorcycle specification, the green section has details of the new owner, and the pink section is sent to the DVLA in the UK when the bike is sold. A small section in yellow deals with selling the bike within the motor trade.

In the UK the DVLA will provide details of earlier keepers of the bike upon payment of a small fee, and much can be learned in this way.

If the bike has a foreign registration there may be expensive and time-consuming formalities to complete. Do you really want the hassle? For European buyers, importing a Harley from the USA might seem tempting – there's bigger choice of bikes, and the climate is usually kinder. However, you'll have to buy the bike sight unseen, and the paperwork to import and re-register is a daunting prospect. That means employing a shipping agent; you'll also have to budget in the shipping costs. Then there's (at the time of writing) 6% import duty on the bike and shipping costs, then 20% VAT on the whole lot. Unless you're after a rare US-only spec bike, it's not worth the hassle.

Roadworthiness certificate

Most country/state administrations require that vehicles are regularly tested to prove they are safe to use on the public highway. In the UK that test (the 'MoT') is carried out at approved testing stations, for a fee. Across the USA the requirement varies, but most states insist on an emissions test every two years as a minimum, while the police are charged with pulling over unsafe-looking vehicles.

In the UK the test is required on an annual basis once a vehicle becomes three years old. Of particular relevance for older bikes is that the certificate issued includes the mileage reading recorded at the test date and, therefore, becomes an independent record of that bike's history. Ask the seller if previous certificates are available. Without an MoT the vehicle should be taken on a flat-bed to its new home, unless you insist that a valid MoT is part of the deal. (Not such a bad idea this – at least you'll know the bike was roadworthy on the day it was tested, and you don't need to wait for the old certificate to expire before having the test done.)

Road licence
The administration of every country/state charges some kind of tax for the use of its roads; the actual form of the 'road licence' and how it's displayed, varies enormously from country-to-country and state-to-state.

Whatever the form, the road licence must relate to the vehicle carrying it, and must be present and valid if the bike is to be driven on the public highway legally. The value of the licence will depend on the length of time it's valid for.

In the UK, if a bike is untaxed because it has not been used for a period of time, the owner must inform the licensing authorities, otherwise the vehicle's date-related registration number will be lost, and there will be a painful amount of paperwork to get it re-registered.

Service history
This is a valuable record, and the more of it there is, the better. The ultimate consists of every single routine service bill (from official Harley dealers, or known and respected independents), plus bills for all other repairs and accessories.

But really, anything helps in the great authenticity game – items like the original bill of sale, handbook, parts invoices and repair bills, all add to the story and character of the machine. Even a brochure correct to the year of the bike's manufacture is a useful document, and something that you could well have to search hard to locate in future years. If the seller claims that the bike has been restored, then expect receipts and other evidence from a specialist restorer.

If the bike has a patchy or non-existent service history, then it could still be perfectly good, but the lack of history should be reflected in the price. Many owners are competent mechanics and look after the bike themselves, but late-model Harleys are increasingly maintained by the local dealer rather than at home.

Restoration photographs
If the seller says the bike has been restored, then expect to be shown a series of photographs taken during the restoration. Pictures taken at various stages and angles, should help you gauge the thoroughness of the work. If you buy the bike, ask if you can have all the photographs, as they form an important part of its history.Many sellers are happy to part with their bike and accept your cash, but want to hang on to their photographs! If so, you may be able to persuade the vendor to get a set of copies made.

Recalls
H-D operates a thorough system of recalls through its dealers, to correct any inherent faults that surface from time to time. All bikes should have been caught in the net, with letters to registered owners asking them to visit a local dealer for rectification work, but it's worth checking the service history to ensure that work has been done. US riders can go to www.nhsta.gov and click 'Recalls' to find out if the bike they're looking at was subject to any recalls (the US National Highway Traffic Safety Administration oversees recalls). UK buyers go to www.vosa.gov.uk/vosa/apps/recalls. Examples are 1999/2000 FLTs (stalling at speed due to the bank angle sensor cutting the ignition off) and 2007 Wide Glides (the bars can crack around a hole for wiring to exit).

12 What's it worth?
– let your head rule your heart

Condition

If the bike you've been looking at is really ratty, you've probably not bothered to use the marking system in chapter 9 (30 minute evaluation). You may not have even got as far as using that chapter at all!

If you did use the marking system in chapter 9 you'll know whether the bike is in Excellent (maybe concours), Good, Average or Poor condition or, perhaps, somewhere in between these categories.

To keep up to date with prices, buy the latest editions of the bike magazines (both Harley specialists and the general bike mags), and check the classified and dealer ads – these are particularly useful as they enable you to compare private and dealer prices. Some of the magazines run auction reports as well, which publish the actual selling prices, as do the auction house websites. Most of the dealers will have up to date websites as well.

Harley values are fairly stable, with slow depreciation after the first 2-3 years, but some bikes will always be more sought after than others. See page 22 for examples of rarer bikes that may appreciate in the future. Think about what you want to do with the bike. For Sunday cruising, there's a lot to be said for a Softail; an Electra or Road Glide will always be the ultimate choice for long distance touring; FXR/Dyna Glide is a good choice if you want an adaptable, all-year round bike.

Assuming that the bike you have in mind is not in show/concours condition, then relate the level of condition that you judge it to be in with the appropriate price in the adverts. How does the figure compare with the asking price? And don't forget that quality accessories can actually increase the value.

Absolute originality isn't a big deal for most Harley owners, as many see the standard bike as a starting point, to be personalised to their taste. By the same token, don't be put off if the bike has pipes, a seat or a tank (or other bolt-on bits) that you don't like. These can always be changed later on, though that will add to the cost and needs to be taken into account when considering what the bike is worth to you.

If you are buying from a dealer, remember there will be a dealer's premium on the price.

Striking a deal

Negotiate on the basis of your condition assessment, mileage, and fault rectification cost. Also take into account the bike's specification. Be realistic about the value, but don't be completely intractable: a small compromise on the part of the vendor or buyer will often facilitate a deal at little real cost.

13 Do you really want to restore?

– it'll take longer and cost more than you think

There's a romance about restoration projects, about bringing a sick bike back to blooming health, and it's tempting to buy something that 'just needs a few small jobs' to bring it up to scratch. But there are two things to think about. One, once you've got the bike home and started taking it apart, those few small jobs could turn into big ones. Two, restoration takes time, which is a precious thing in itself. Be honest with yourself – will you get as much pleasure from working on the bike as you will from riding it?

Let's just add here that you are unlikely to find an Evo or Twin Cam Harley that needs a total restoration. Even though the oldest Evos have been around for over 25 years, most have been looked after by previous owners, kept in dry garages and

Fully restored '85 Electra, or a brand new one? Neither option is cheap.

haven't suffered from much winter weather. When did you last see a tatty late-model Harley? It's true there are some riders who really do use their bikes all year round and aren't too bothered about cosmetics. Even they are often knowledgeable types who will have kept the bike well up to scratch mechanically.

Still, there are always exceptions, so let's assume that you have found a bike, maybe at a bargain price, that needs a great deal of work to get it back on the road. You could hand the whole lot over to a professional, and the biggest cost involved there is not the new parts, but the sheer labour involved. Such restorations don't come cheap, and if taking this route there are four other issues to bear in mind as well.

First, make it absolutely clear what you want doing. Do you want the bike to be 100% original at the end of the process, or simply useable? Do you want a concours finish, or are you prepared to put up with a few blemishes on the original parts?

Secondly, make sure that not only is a detailed estimate involved, but that it is more or less binding. There are too many stories of a person quoted one figure only to be presented with an invoice for a far larger one!

Third, check that the company you're dealing with has a good reputation – the owners' club, or one of the reputable parts suppliers, should be able to make a few recommendations. Finally, the restoration cost will rarely be covered by the bike's subsequent value, except maybe in the future for some rare models.

Restoring a Harley yourself requires a number of skills, which is fine if you already have them, but if you haven't it's good not to make your newly acquired bike part of the learning curve! Can you weld? Are you confident about building up an engine? Do you have a warm, well-lit garage with a solid workbench and a good selection of tools?

Be prepared for a top-notch professional to put you on a lengthy waiting list, or, if tackling a restoration yourself, expect things to go wrong and set aside extra time to complete the task. Restorations can stretch into years when things like life intrude, so it's good to have some sort of target date.

A rolling restoration has much to recommend it, especially as the summers start to pass with your bike still off the road. This is not the way to achieve a concours finish, which can only really be achieved via a thorough nut-and-bolt rebuild, without the bike getting wet and dirty in the meantime. But there's a lot to be said for a rolling restoration. Riding helps keep your interest up as the bike's condition improves, and it's also more affordable than trying to do everything in one go. It will take longer, but you'll get some on-road fun out of the bike in the meantime.

14 Paint problems
– bad complexion, including dimples, pimples and bubbles

Paint faults generally occur due to lack of protection and/or maintenance, or to poor preparation prior to a repaint or touch-up. Some of the following conditions may be present in the bike you're looking at.

Orange peel
This appears as an uneven paint surface, similar to the appearance of the skin of an orange. The fault is caused by the failure of atomized paint droplets to flow into each other when they hit the surface. It's sometimes possible to rub out the effect with proprietary paint cutting/rubbing compound, or very fine grades of abrasive paper. A respray may be necessary in severe cases. Consult a bodywork repairer/paint shop for advice.

Cracking
Severe cases are likely to have been caused by too heavy an application of paint (or filler beneath the paint). Also, insufficient stirring of the paint before application can lead to the components being improperly mixed, and cracking can result. Incompatibility with the paint already on the panel can have a similar effect.
To rectify it's necessary to rub down to a smooth, sound finish before respraying the problem area.

Crazing
Sometimes the paint takes on a crazed rather than a cracked appearance when the problems mentioned under 'Cracking' are present. This problem can also be caused by a reaction between the underlying surface and the paint. Paint removal and respraying the problem area is usually the only solution.

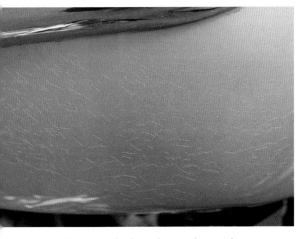

A respray is the only cure for crazing.

Blistering
Almost always caused by corrosion of the metal beneath the paint. Perforation will usually be found in the metal, and the damage will be worse than that suggested by the area of blistering. The metal will have to be repaired before repainting.

Micro blistering
Usually the result of an economy respray where inadequate heating has allowed moisture to

settle on the vehicle before spraying. Consult a paint specialist, but damaged paint will have to be removed before partial or full respraying. Can also be caused by bike covers that don't 'breathe.'

Fading
Some colours, especially solid reds, are prone to fading if subject to strong sunlight for long periods without polish protection. Sometimes proprietary paint restorers and/or paint cutting/rubbing compounds will retrieve the situation. Often a respray is the only real solution.

Peeling
Often a problem with metallic paintwork starts when the sealing lacquer becomes damaged and begins to peel off. Poorly applied paint may also peel. The remedy is to strip and start again!

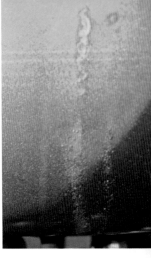

Blisters are caused by corrosion.

Dimples
Dimples in the paintwork are caused by a residue of polish (particularly silicone types) not being removed properly before respraying. Paint removal and repainting is the only solution.

If buying a bike with custom paint, can you live with it?

15 Problems due to lack of use
– just like their owners, Harleys need exercise!

Like any piece of engineering, and indeed like human beings, Harley Big Twins deterioriate if they sit doing nothing for long periods. This is especially relevant if the bike is laid up for six months of the year, as some of these bikes are.

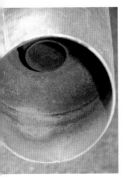

Damp storage leads to this.

Rust
If the bike is put away wet, and/or stored in a cold, damp garage, the paint, metal and brightwork will suffer. Ensure the machine is completely dry and clean before going into storage, and if you can afford it, invest in a dehumidifier to keep the garage atmosphere dry.

Seized components
Pistons in brake calipers can seize partially or fully, giving binding or non-working brakes. Cables are vulnerable to seizure too – the answer is to thoroughly lube them beforehand, and come into the garage to give them a couple of pulls once a week or so.

Calipers will eventually begin to seize.

Tyres
When the bike is parked up, most of its weight is on the tyres, which will develop flat spots and cracks over time. The only long-term answer is to put the bike up on blocks.

Engine
Old, acidic oil can corrode bearings. Many riders change the oil in the spring, when they're putting the bike back on the road, but really it should be changed just before the bike is laid up, so that the bearings are sitting in fresh oil. The same goes for the gearbox. While you're giving the cables their weekly exercise, turn the engine over slowly on the kickstart, if there is one, with the ignition off. Don't start it though – running the engine for a short time does more harm than good, as it produces a lot of moisture internally, which the engine doesn't get hot enough to burn off. That will attack the engine internals, and the silencers.

Tyres will crack and degrade, though it takes a long time.

Battery/electrics
Either remove the battery and give it a top-up charge every couple of weeks, or connect it up to a battery top-up device such as the Optimate, which will keep it permanently fully charged. Damp conditions will allow fuses and earth connections to corrode, storing up electrical troubles for the spring. Eventually, wiring insulation will harden and fail.

16 The Community
– key people, organisations and companies in the Harley world

Clubs across the world

All Harley owners benefit from the biggest, most extensive official club network there is – the Harley Owners Group, or HOG, which is run by the factory and mostly based at local dealers.

There are local chapters of HOG all over the world, and every one of them has an active social calendar. They're a great way to meet other Harley owners that live close to you.

There are well-established independent clubs as well, with long experience of the big V-twins, and much technical knowledge. Either way, there isn't room here to list them all, but here's a good selection.

HOG branches by country

Below is just a small sample of countries with HOG chapters: the Harley-Davidson website (www.harley-davidson.com) has a 'Find a HOG chapter' facility, where you can search for a chapter either by country or location.

Australia
Austria
Belgium
Canada
France
Germany
Japan
Mexico
Netherlands
New Zealand
Spain
Switzerland
United Kingdom
USA

Independent clubs

Federation of Harley-Davidson Clubs Europe – www.fhdce.eu
Harley-Davidson Club of Denmark – www.hdc.dk
Harley-Davidson Club Nederland – www.h-dcn.nl
Harley-Davidson Italian Club – www.h-dic.com
Harley-Davidson Riders Club of GB – www.hdrcgb.com

Specialists

There are so many Harley specialists out there that it would be impossible to list them all, so I have restricted the listing to some UK companies. To find your official local Harley dealer, go to www.harley-davidson.com

All-American Motorcycles – Worcestershire
www.allamc.co.uk – 01299 251 111

Andy Harris Custom Cycles – Essex
www.harley-tech.com – 01621 841 114

B & H Motorcycles – Cornwall
www.bnh-motorcycles.co.uk – 01726 824 256

James Retro Ltd – Middlesex
www.james-retro.com – 01784 421 700

John Wynne Automotive – Cheshire
www.jwautomotive.net – 0151 334 3233

Le Rock – Nottinghamshire
www.le-rock-ltd.co.uk – 01623 632 266

Milwaukee Motorcycle Co – Kent
www.mmc-bikes.com – 01892 538 102

V-Twin Mania – Edinburgh
www.vtwinmania.com – 0131 622 0031

Books

There are more books about Harleys than any other bike. Here is a very small selection:

Harley-Davidson Since 1965, Allan Girdler
Harley-Davidson Motorcycles: All You Need To Know, Bill Stermer
The Complete Harley-Davidson, Tod Rafferty
Encyclopedia of the Harley-Davidson, Peter Henshaw
SpeedPro™ Series: How to Power Tune Harley-Davidson 1340 Evolution Engines, Des Hammill

17 Vital statistics
– essential data at your fingertips

Listing the vital statistics of every Big Twin variant would take far more room than we have here, so we've picked three representative models: 1984 FLHTC, 1991 Dyna Daytona and 2007 Fat Boy.

Max speed
1984 FLHTC – 96mph
1991 Dyna Daytona – 101mph
2007 Fat Boy – 110mph

Engine
1984 FLHTC – Air-cooled 45-degree V-twin Evolution, 1339cc, bore and stroke
   88.8 x 108mm, compression ratio 8.5:1, 82.5lb ft @ 3600rpm
1991 Dyna Daytona – Air-cooled 45-degree V-twin Evolution, 1339cc, bore and
   stroke 88.8 x 108mm, compression ratio 8.5:1, 83lb ft @ 4000rpm
2007 Fat Boy – Air-cooled 45-degree V-twin Twin Cam TC96B, 1584cc, bore and
   stroke, 95.3 x 111.1mm, compression ratio 9.2:1, 89lb ft @ 3300rpm

Gearbox
1984 FLHTC – Five-speed. Ratios: 1st 10.45:1, 7.13:1, 5.17:1, 3.98:1, 3.22:1
1991 Dyna Daytona – Five-speed. Ratios: n/a
2007 Fat Boy – Six-speed. Ratios 1st 9.31:1, 6.42:1, 4.77:1, 3.93:1, 3.28:1, 2.79:1

Final drive
1984 FLHTC – Fully enclosed chain
1991 Dyna Daytona – Toothed belt
2007 Fat Boy – Toothed belt

Brakes
1984 FLHTC – Front: 2 x discs, 2-pot calipers; rear: 1 x disc, 2-pot caliper
1991 Dyna Daytona – Front: 2 x discs, 2-pot calipers; rear: 1 x disc, 2-pot caliper
2007 Fat Boy – Front: 1 x disc, 4-pot caliper; rear: 1x disc, 4-pot caliper

Electrics
1984 FLHTC – 12v, 264w alternator
1991 Dyna Daytona – 12v, 360w alternator
2007 Fat Boy – 12v, 489w alternator

Weight
1984 FLHTC – 346kg (dry)
1991 Dyna Daytona – 278kg (with half-tank fuel)
2007 Fat Boy – 313kg (dry)

Model introductions by model years

1984 – Evolution engine launched; Softail, Sport Glide, police-spec Pursuit Glide

1985 – FXRs get Evolution, toothed belt for Tourers; Low Glide Custom and Disc Glide

1986 – Heritage Softail, FXR Super Glide, Softail Custom; Low Glide becomes Low Rider

1987 – Electra Glide Sport, Low Rider Sport

1988 – Springer Softail

1989 – Heritage Softail Classic, Convertible, Electra Glide Ultra

1990 – Fat Boy

1991 – Dyna Glide chassis (32-degree rake), Sturgis

1992 – Dyna Daytona and Dyna Custom

1993 – 'Cow Glide' (this year only), Dyna Low Rider and Wide Glide

1994 – Road King, Heritage Softail Nostalgia

1995 – 30th Anniversary Ultra Classic Electra Glide, with fuel-injection, revised Dyna chassis (28-degree rake), Dyna Convertible, Bad Boy, Electra Glide Standard

1996 – Injection option extends to more tourers

1997 – Heritage Springer Softail

1998 – Night Train, Road King Classic

1999 – Twin Cam (TC88) fitted to Touring and Dyna ranges

2000 – TC88B balanced engine fitted to Softails; Softail Deuce

2001 – Fuel-injection for Softails; Super Glide T-Sport

2002 – Electra Glide Classic returns

2004 – Road King Custom

2005 – Softail Deluxe; last year for carburettor bikes

2006 – Cruise Drive six-speed gearbox on Dyna Glides, Dyna Street Bob, and Street Glide

2007 – Cruise Drive fitted to Touring and Softails, TC96 introduced, 110in^3 engine on CVO models

2009 – Touring range has new frame and revised engine mountings; Dyna Street Bob and Fat Bob, Softail Cross Bones and Rocker

Model codes (FXR/FL models only)

BH = FXST
BJ = FLSTC
BK = FXSTC
BL = FXSTS
BM = FLSTF
BN = FLSTN
BP = FXSTSB
BR = FLSTS
BS = FXSTD
BT = FXSTB
DA = FLT 82-83
DA = FLHTP police windshield
DB = FLTC
DC = FLHT
DD = FLHT
DE = FLHTC w/sidecar
DF = FLHTP police fairing
DG = FLHTC shrine
DH = FLTC w/sidecar

DJ = FLHTC
DK = FLTC shrine
DM = FLTCU
DP = FLHTCU
EA = FXR
EB = FXRS
EC = FXRT
ED = FXRP police windshield
EF = FXRP police fairing
EG = FXRS-SP
EJ = FXRC
EH = FXRD
EK = FXRP police CHP
EL = FXLR
EM = FXLR conv
FA = FLHS
FB = FLHR-I
FC = FLHTCU-I
FD = FLHR

FE = FLTCU-I
FF = FLHTC-I
FG = FLHTCU-I w/sc
FH = FLHP-I police
FJ = FLHP police
FL = FLHTCU-I shrine
FM = FLHTP-I police
FP = FLTR
FR = FLHRC-I
FS = FLTR-I
FT = FLHPE-I (California)
GA = FXDB-D
GB = FXDB-S
GC = FXDC
GD = FXDL
GE = FXDWG
GG = FXDS conv
GH = FXD
SG = TLE police
SH = RLE police

The **Essential** Buyer's Guide™ series

The Essential Buyer's Guide
BUS
978-1-845840-22-8

The Essential Buyer's Guide
TR6
978-1-845840-26-6

The Essential Buyer's Guide
MGB MGB GT
978-1-845840-29-7

The Essential Buyer's Guide
E-type
978-1-845840-77-8

The Essential Buyer's Guide
2CV
978-1-845840-99-0

The Essential Buyer's Guide
MINOR & 1000
978-1-845841-01-0

The Essential Buyer's Guide
280-560SL & SLC
978-1-845841-07-2

The Essential Buyer's Guide
230, 250 & 280SL
978-1-845841-13-3

The Essential Buyer's Guide
XJ6, XJ12 & Sovereign
978-1-845841-19-5

The Essential Buyer's Guide
BONNEVILLE
978-1-845841-34-8

The Essential Buyer's Guide
GS
978-1-845841-35-5

The Essential Buyer's Guide
500, 650 Twins
978-1-845841-36-2

The Essential Buyer's Guide
DS & ID
978-1-845841-38-6

The Essential Buyer's Guide
SILVER SHADOW T-SERIES
978-1-845841-46-1

The Essential Buyer's Guide
500 & 600
978-1-845841-47-8

The Essential Buyer's Guide
XJ-S
978-1-845841-61-4

The Essential Buyer's Guide
IMPREZA
978-1-845841-63-8

The Essential Buyer's Guide
Bantam
978-1-845841-65-2

The Essential Buyer's Guide
GOLF GTI
978-1-845841-88-1

The Essential Buyer's Guide
XJ40
978-1-845841-92-8

The Essential Buyer's Guide
XJ
978-1-845842-00-0

The Essential Buyer's Guide
MINI
978-1-845842-04-8

The Essential Buyer's Guide
CAPRI
978-1-845842-05-5

The Essential Buyer's Guide
STAG
978-1-845842-70-3

The Essential Buyer's Guide
Commando
978-1-845842-81-9

The Essential Buyer's Guide
205 GTI
978-1-845842-83-3

The Essential Buyer's Guide
SOHC FOURS
978-1-845842-84-0

The Essential Buyer's Guide
TRIPLES & FOURS
978-1-845842-87-1

The Essential Buyer's Guide
Z3
978-1-845842-90-1

The Essential Buyer's Guide
Big Twins
978-1-845843-03-8

The Essential Buyer's Guide
CBR FireBlade
978-1-845843-07-6

The Essential Buyer's Guide
CBR600 HURRICANE
978-1-845843-09-0

The Essential Buyer's Guide
TR7 & TR8
978-1-845843-16-8

The Essential Buyer's Guide
CORVETTE
978-1-845843-29-8

The Essential Buyer's Guide
911SC
978-1-845843-30-4

The Essential Buyer's Guide
SCOOTERS
978-1-845843-34-2

The Essential Buyer's Guide
911 (964)
978-1-845843-38-0

The Essential Buyer's Guide
911 (996)
978-1-845843-39-7

The Essential Buyer's Guide
911 (993)
978-1-845843-40-3

The Essential Buyer's Guide
SERIES I, II & IIA
978-1-845843-48-9

The Essential Buyer's Guide
TD, TF & TF1500
978-1-845843-52-6

The Essential Buyer's Guide
SEVEN
978-1-845843-53-3

The Essential Buyer's Guide
MIDGET & SPRITE
978-1-845843-54-0

The Essential Buyer's Guide
Spitfire & GT6
978-1-845843-56-4

The Essential Buyer's Guide
XK8
978-1-845843-59-5

The Essential Buyer's Guide
Mk II
978-1-845843-60-1

The Essential Buyer's Guide
E21 3 Series
978-1-845843-66-3

The Essential Buyer's Guide
Replicas
978-1-845843-95-3

The Essential Buyer's Guide
GT COUPÉ
978-1-904788-69-0

The Essential Buyer's Guide
928
978-1-904788-70-6

The Essential Buyer's Guide
BEETLE
978-1-904788-72-0

The Essential Buyer's Guide
E-type
978-1-904788-85-0

The Essential Buyer's Guide
SPIDER
978-1-904788-98-0

£9.99*/$19.95*

*prices subject to change, p&p extra.
For more details visit www.veloce.co.uk
or email info@veloce.co.uk

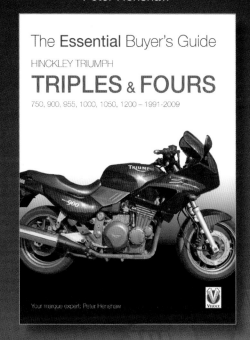

The Essential Buyer's Guide™
Honda CBR FireBlade
Peter Henshaw

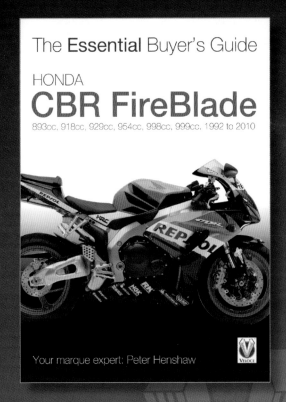

The **Essential** Buyer's Guide

HONDA
CBR FireBlade
893cc, 918cc, 929cc, 954cc, 998cc, 999cc. 1992 to 2010

Your marque expert: Peter Henshaw

ISBN 978-1-845843-07-6
Paperback • 19.5x13.9cm • £9.99* UK / $19.95* US
• 64 pages • 84 pictures

Having this book in your pocket is just like having a real marque expert
by your side. Benefit from Peter Henshaw's years of experience, learn
how to spot a bad bike quickly, and how to assess a promising one like a
professional. Get the right bike at the right price!
Packed with good advice – from running costs, through paperwork, vital
statistics, valuation, and the CBR FireBlade community, to whether a CBR
FireBlade will suit you and your lifestyle – this is the complete guide to
choosing, assessing and buying the CBR FireBlade of your dreams.